DATE DUE

AG 3'98			
MR 03 00			
MR 1'11			

DEMCO 38-297

WHOOPI
GOLDBERG

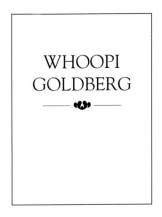

WHOOPI GOLDBERG

Rose Blue
and
Corinne J. Naden

CHELSEA HOUSE PUBLISHERS
New York   Philadelphia

The authors gratefully acknowledge the cooperation of Ms. Whoopi Goldberg, who graciously provided a personal interview for this volume. They also wish to thank Mr. Brad Cafarelli of Bragman Nyman Cafarelli for his generous assistance.

Dedication: From Corinne, to Claire and Gloria, my show-biz buddies.
From Rose, to my friend Marty Winkler, Mr. Show Business.

Chelsea House Publishers
Editorial Director Richard Rennert
Executive Managing Editor Karyn Gullen Browne
Copy Chief Robin James
Picture Editor Adrian G. Allen
Art Director Robert Mitchell
Manufacturing Director Gerald Levine
Assistant Art Director Joan Ferrigno

Black Americans of Achievement
Senior Editor Philip Koslow

Staff for WHOOPI GOLDBERG
Copy Editor Catherine Iannone
Editorial Assistant Sydra Mallery
Designer John Infantino
Picture Researcher Ellen Barrett Dudley
Cover Illustrator Janet Hamlin

3 5 7 9 8 6 4 2

Library of Congress Cataloging-in-Publication Data
Blue, Rose.
    Whoopi Goldberg: entertainer / Rose Blue and Corinne J. Naden
        p. cm. — (Black Americans of achievement)
    Includes bibliographical references and index.
    ISBN 0-7910-2152-1.
        0-7910-2153-X (pbk.)
    1. Goldberg, Whoopi, 1950– —Juvenile literature. 2. Comedians—United States—Biography—Juvenile literature. 3. Afro-American Comedians—United States—Biography—Juvenile literature. 4. Motion picture actors and actresses—United States—Biography—Juvenile literature. [1. Goldberg, Whoopi, 1950– . 2. Comedians. 3. Actors and actresses. 4. Afro-Americans—Biography. 5. Women—Biography.] I. Naden, Corinne J. II. Title. III. Series.
PN2287 .G578B58 1994   94-17344
791'.43'028'092—dc20   CIP
[B]   AC

Frontispiece: Whoopi Goldberg, photographed in 1984, when her talents as an actress and comedian were propelling her to stardom.

CONTENTS

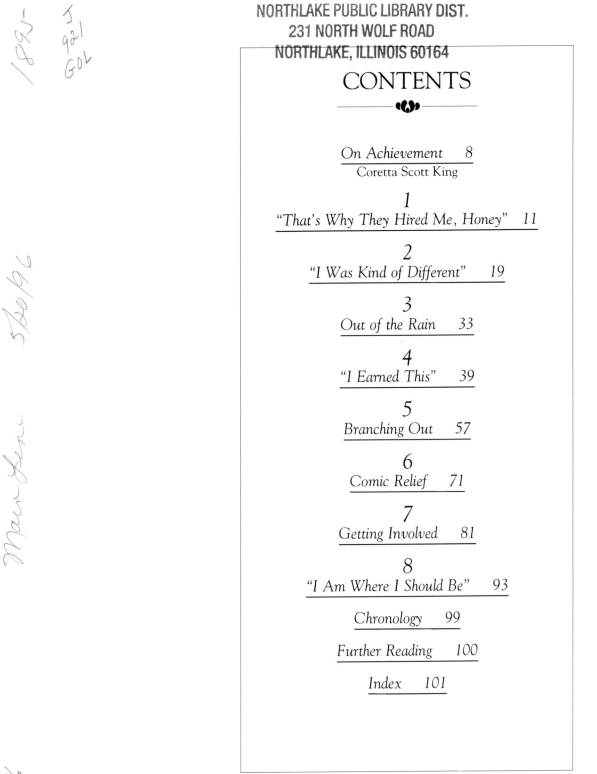

BLACK AMERICANS OF ACHIEVEMENT

HENRY AARON
baseball great

KAREEM ABDUL-JABBAR
basketball great

RALPH ABERNATHY
civil rights leader

ALVIN AILEY
choreographer

MUHAMMAD ALI
heavyweight champion

RICHARD ALLEN
*religious leader and
social activist*

MAYA ANGELOU
author

LOUIS ARMSTRONG
musician

ARTHUR ASHE
tennis great

JOSEPHINE BAKER
entertainer

JAMES BALDWIN
author

BENJAMIN BANNEKER
scientist and mathematician

AMIRI BARAKA
poet and playwright

COUNT BASIE
bandleader and composer

ROMARE BEARDEN
artist

JAMES BECKWOURTH
frontiersman

MARY MCLEOD BETHUNE
educator

JULIAN BOND
civil rights leader and politician

GWENDOLYN BROOKS
poet

JIM BROWN
football great

RALPH BUNCHE
diplomat

STOKELY CARMICHAEL
civil rights leader

GEORGE WASHINGTON
CARVER
botanist

RAY CHARLES
musician

CHARLES CHESNUTT
author

JOHN COLTRANE
musician

BILL COSBY
entertainer

PAUL CUFFE
merchant and abolitionist

COUNTEE CULLEN
poet

BENJAMIN DAVIS, SR., AND
BENJAMIN DAVIS, JR.
military leaders

SAMMY DAVIS, JR.
entertainer

FATHER DIVINE
religious leader

FREDERICK DOUGLASS
abolitionist editor

CHARLES DREW
physician

W. E. B. DU BOIS
scholar and activist

PAUL LAURENCE DUNBAR
poet

KATHERINE DUNHAM
dancer and choreographer

DUKE ELLINGTON
bandleader and composer

RALPH ELLISON
author

JULIUS ERVING
basketball great

JAMES FARMER
civil rights leader

ELLA FITZGERALD
singer

MARCUS GARVEY
black nationalist leader

JOSH GIBSON
baseball great

DIZZY GILLESPIE
musician

WHOOPI GOLDBERG
entertainer

ALEX HALEY
author

PRINCE HALL
social reformer

MATTHEW HENSON
explorer

CHESTER HIMES
author

BILLIE HOLIDAY
singer

LENA HORNE
entertainer

LANGSTON HUGHES
poet

ZORA NEALE HURSTON
author

JESSE JACKSON
civil rights leader and politician

MICHAEL JACKSON
entertainer

JACK JOHNSON
heavyweight champion

JAMES WELDON JOHNSON
author

MAGIC JOHNSON
basketball great

SCOTT JOPLIN
composer

BARBARA JORDAN
politician

MICHAEL JORDAN
basketball great

CORETTA SCOTT KING
civil rights leader

MARTIN LUTHER KING, JR.
civil rights leader

LEWIS LATIMER
scientist

SPIKE LEE
filmmaker

CARL LEWIS
champion athlete

JOE LOUIS
heavyweight champion

RONALD MCNAIR
astronaut

MALCOLM X
militant black leader

THURGOOD MARSHALL
Supreme Court justice

TONI MORRISON
author

ELIJAH MUHAMMAD
religious leader

EDDIE MURPHY
entertainer

JESSE OWENS
champion athlete

SATCHEL PAIGE
baseball great

CHARLIE PARKER
musician

GORDON PARKS
photographer

ROSA PARKS
civil rights leader

SIDNEY POITIER
actor

ADAM CLAYTON
POWELL, JR.
political leader

COLIN POWELL
military leader

LEONTYNE PRICE
opera singer

A. PHILIP RANDOLPH
labor leader

PAUL ROBESON
singer and actor

JACKIE ROBINSON
baseball great

DIANA ROSS
entertainer

BILL RUSSELL
basketball great

JOHN RUSSWURM
publisher

SOJOURNER TRUTH
antislavery activist

HARRIET TUBMAN
antislavery activist

NAT TURNER
slave revolt leader

DENMARK VESEY
slave revolt leader

ALICE WALKER
author

MADAM C. J. WALKER
entrepreneur

BOOKER T. WASHINGTON
educator and racial spokesman

IDA WELLS-BARNETT
civil rights leader

WALTER WHITE
civil rights leader

OPRAH WINFREY
entertainer

STEVIE WONDER
musician

RICHARD WRIGHT
author

ON ACHIEVEMENT

Coretta Scott King

BEFORE YOU BEGIN this book, I hope you will ask yourself what the word *excellence* means to you. I think that it's a question we should all ask, and keep asking as we grow older and change. Because the truest answer to it should never change. When you think of excellence, perhaps you think of success at work; or of becoming wealthy; or meeting the right person, getting married, and having a good family life.

Those important goals are worth striving for, but there is a better way to look at excellence. As Martin Luther King, Jr., said in one of his last sermons, "I want you to be first in love. I want you to be first in moral excellence. I want you to be first in generosity. If you want to be important, wonderful. If you want to be great, wonderful. But recognize that he who is greatest among you shall be your servant."

My husband, Martin Luther King, Jr., knew that the true meaning of achievement is service. When I met him, in 1952, he was already ordained as a Baptist preacher and was working toward a doctoral degree at Boston University. I was studying at the New England Conservatory and dreamed of accomplishments in music. We married a year later, and after I graduated the following year we moved to Montgomery, Alabama. We didn't know it then, but our notions of achievement were about to undergo a dramatic change.

You may have read or heard about what happened next. What began with the boycott of a local bus line grew into a national movement, and by the time he was assassinated in 1968 my husband had fashioned a black movement powerful enough to shatter forever the practice of racial segregation. What you may not have read about is where he got his method for resisting injustice without compromising his religious beliefs.

He adopted the strategy of nonviolence from a man of a different race, who lived in a different country, and even practiced a different religion. The man was Mahatma Gandhi, the great leader of India, who devoted his life to serving humanity in the spirit of love and nonviolence. It was in these principles that Martin discovered his method for social reform. More than anything else, those two principles were the key to his achievements.

This book is about black Americans who served society through the excellence of their achievements. It forms a part of the rich history of black men and women in America—a history of stunning accomplishments in every field of human endeavor, from literature and art to science, industry, education, diplomacy, athletics, jurisprudence, even polar exploration.

Not all of the people in this history had the same ideals, but I think you will find something that all of them had in common. Like Martin Luther King, Jr., they all decided to become "drum majors" and serve humanity. In that principle—whether it was expressed in books, inventions, or song—they found something outside themselves to use as a goal and a guide. Something that showed them a way to serve others, instead of only living for themselves.

Reading the stories of these courageous men and women not only helps us discover the principles that we will use to guide our own lives but also teaches us about our black heritage and about America itself. It is crucial for us to know the heroes and heroines of our history and to realize that the price we paid in our struggle for equality in America was dear. But we must also understand that we have gotten as far as we have partly because America's democratic system and ideals made it possible.

We are still struggling with racism and prejudice. But the great men and women in this series are a tribute to the spirit of our democratic ideals and the system in which they have flourished. And that makes their stories special and worth knowing. ❧

1

"THAT'S WHY THEY HIRED ME, HONEY"

O N THE EVENING of March 21, 1994, a star-studded audience gathered in the Dorothy Chandler Pavilion of the Los Angeles Music Center for the 66th annual Academy Awards ceremonies. The Academy Awards, popularly known as the Oscars, are presented by the Academy of Motion Picture Arts and Sciences to honor the year's outstanding achievements in the American film industry. One of the great rituals in American culture, the Oscars give the public a chance to see their favorite movie stars off the screen, parading in tuxedos and glittering gowns, speaking their own words as they accept or present awards, or merely sitting in the audience as though they were ordinary people on a night out.

The role of host at the Academy Awards gala, which is televised into hundreds of millions of homes throughout the world, is one of the great plums in the world of show business. For many years, the comedian Bob Hope presided over the festivities, making wisecracks about Hollywood and joking about his own failure ever to win an Oscar. More recently, another highly successful comedian, Billy Crystal, starred in the emcee's role for four years.

The first female host in the history of the Academy Awards, Goldberg greets the star-studded audience on March 21, 1994. During the course of the evening, Goldberg lived up to her reputation as a charming, hilarious, and sometimes controversial personality.

11

After the 1993 ceremonies, however, Crystal decided that he had done his last Oscar night, and the producers began to search for a replacement. Their final choice was something of a surprise, delighting some and worrying others. As March 22 approached, the film industry and the public were prepared for an unusual experience.

The ceremonies opened with a brief speech by Arthur Hiller, the president of the Academy of Motion Picture Arts and Sciences, followed by a filmed musical tribute to the technicians who do the nuts-and-bolts work of creating motion pictures. Then the amplified voice of the public-address announcer rang out over the packed auditorium: "And now, ladies and gentlemen, your host for the 66th annual Academy Awards—Whoopi Goldberg!"

Dressed in a floor-length brown velvet gown, Whoopi Goldberg swept to the front of the stage, wearing a typically mischievous grin on her round, expressive face. The audience welcomed her warmly, paying tribute to her unquestioned status as a Hollywood star—she had herself won an Oscar in 1991 But they also knew her well-earned reputation for outspokenness. She was likely to say anything, no matter what the occasion, no matter how many people were watching, no matter who was likely to be offended. Some of the assembled personalities were delighted at the prospect of Goldberg's doing something outrageous; others cringed at the thought that she might stir up some controversy that would overshadow the glamour of the Oscars.

Beaming in acknowledgment of the applause, Goldberg immediately addressed the contradictory feelings swirling around her. "So, they went and gave me a live mike for three hours," she said with a wicked smile. Enjoying the mixed emotions surrounding her appearance, Goldberg pointed out with some pride that she was the first woman ever to host the Academy Awards. "I want to put a rumor to rest," she went on. "I did not get this gig because I'm Sidney Poitier's daughter. I got it because I seem to cross so many ethnic and political lines. I'm an equal opportunity offender."

When the laughter died down, she made a pointed reference to the many political speeches at the previous year's Oscar ceremonies. "And to make sure you don't feel shortchanged in the political soapbox department, I'm gonna get it all out of my system right now." At this point, she reeled off a string of political slogans: "Save the whales, save the spotted owl, men's rights, women's rights, human rights, feed the homeless, more gun control. . . ." Just when the audience was beginning to relax, believing that Goldberg was finally sticking to the middle of the road, she dropped in a daring quip that drew roars of laughter from some members of the audience and loud groans from others. "I think I took care of everything," she said in summation. "Including my career."

Midway during the evening, Goldberg shed her elegant image for a funkier and more familiar persona, reappearing onstage in a tuxedo and floppy bow tie. Her hair, which had previously been pinned up, now tumbled about her face in a profusion of dreadlocks. "Come on, you didn't think I was gonna spend all night in that dress, did you?" she cracked. Throughout the evening, she continued to aim her humorous barbs at a variety of targets, including the Los Angeles press, which had often taken a critical view of her actions. "Hey, if I have to take it, I'm going to give it, too," she remarked pointedly. After another joke appeared to upset some

Whoopi Goldberg clutches the Academy Award she won in 1991 for her performance in Ghost. After receiving the film industry's supreme honor, Goldberg became one of the most sought after and highly paid performers in Hollywood.

members of the audience, Goldberg shrugged and once again flashed her impish grin: "That's why they hired me, honey."

During the three-hour telecast, Goldberg more than lived up to her billing. Though it was anyone's guess whether she would be invited back for 1995 and beyond—or whether, indeed, she would care to return—her debut as host was clearly a success. The *New York Times* described her as a "poised and funny host," though the conservative paper added that Goldberg "relied heavily on the kinds of man-ogling jokes that no male host could get away with making about women." Most likely, Goldberg enjoyed reading that comment—she had no objection to getting away with things when she was onstage.

Indeed, at the outset of her career, few people would have supposed that a black woman could get away with calling herself Whoopi Goldberg. The name's owner was far more likely to wind up a trivia question than a full-fledged star. But apart from hard work, Goldberg's entire career—like her performance on Oscar night—had thrived on her ability to surprise.

Goldberg had been born with a thoroughly ordinary name—Caryn Johnson. On her way to stardom, she became Whoopi Goldberg. In an interview for *Playboy* magazine in 1987, she revealed how it happened: "The name was a fluke. A joke. It started when I was doing *A Christmas Carol* in San Diego. We'd sit backstage and talk about names we'd never give our children, like Pork Pie or Independence. Of course, now people *are* walking around with those names. A woman said to me, 'If I was your mother, I would have called you Whoopi, because when you're happy you make a sound like that practical joke whoopee cushion.' It was like 'Ha-ha-ha-ha—

Whoopi!' So people actually started calling me Whoopi Cushion."

Johnson actually adopted Whoopi Cushion as her stage name, a decision that horrified her mother. After living with the name change for several months, Mrs. Johnson told her daughter that no one would take an actress named Whoopi Cushion with any degree of seriousness. Whoopi bowed to her mother's judgment and decided on the last name of Goldberg. At first Whoopi made up a number of stories about why she chose the name Goldberg. The truth just seemed too dull. Then she admitted that the name had been her mother's idea. It just seemed to fit, although she has claimed that it really is the name of one of her mother's relatives.

Goldberg's friends loved the new name, but the critics did not. One critic reviewing a performance wrote: "Whoopi Goldberg was fantastic, but that name is ridiculous." Goldberg wrote the critic a letter and said that a rose by any other name would still be an actor.

New name or not, Goldberg never forgot who she was or where she came from. "When I go out in public," she has said, "I go out as Whoopi Goldberg. But when I'm in the house, it's Caryn Johnson. Caryn Johnson parent. Caryn Johnson grandmother. I take the mask off." Indeed, Goldberg was not pleased when the press discovered her real name, because it brought her stage life too close to her private life. "I was thinking about my daughter," she explained. "I did not want people invading my home, asking questions. I just wanted a little privacy. . . . Couldn't even go to the PTA anymore. So when my real name came out in the press, it teed me off."

Whoopi Goldberg is an invented character, a set of gestures, remarks, and facial expressions. The real-life Caryn Johnson is a woman with a remarkable story, a woman who at the age of 20 had already been through some of life's toughest experiences—the drug scene, welfare, a failed marriage, an infant to care for. But from that woman at that place in that time, there emerged a performer who could stride to the front of a stage with the whole world watching and give Hollywood's elite something to think about. ❦

2

"I WAS KIND OF DIFFERENT"

❦

CARYN JOHNSON arrived in the family of Robert and Emma Harris Johnson on November 13, 1955. Apparently, she came on the New York City scene ready to perform and knowing what she wanted.

"Being a performer was always my destiny," she later said. "I knew what I was meant to be. My mom knew it from day one. When I was born, the doctor didn't have to pop me to get me going. Mom said I was completely ready to live. The first thing I did was stick my thumb in my mouth. It was like 'Thank you. Thank you. I am here.' "

The Johnsons lived in a housing project at 26th Street and 10th Avenue on the West Side of Manhattan, in a neighborhood known as Chelsea. Writing of the neighborhood's great landmark, the Chelsea Hotel (built in 1883), the journalist Pete Hamill described a melting pot that mirrored the entire racially mixed neighborhood: "a place of rednecks in the 1930s, British sailors in the 1940s, beatniks in the 1950s, hippies in the 1960s, and pretenders in the 1970s." Indeed, the area has a colorful history, and the Chelsea Hotel still draws both artists and the arty. The distinguished composer Virgil Thomson lived and worked in the Chelsea for much of his adult life. Woody Allen used the hotel

Goldberg's pensive expression in this scene from the 1988 film The Telephone *reveals another aspect of her dramatic talent and also reflects the struggles she endured on her way to stardom.*

A view of New York's
legendary Chelsea Hotel during
the mid-1960s. Growing up in
the racially mixed and artistically
vibrant Chelsea neighborhood,
Goldberg was exposed to both
exciting possibilities and
dangerous temptations.

for some scenes in his film *Manhattan Murder Mystery,* and Madonna staged a photo shoot at the Chelsea. Teenagers still go to the front desk to request a visit to the room used by rocker Sid Vicious of the Sex Pistols. The neighborhood surrounding the hotel is equally filled with contrasts. Elegant brownstones alternate with run-down tenements and low-income housing projects such as the one the Johnsons lived in.

Goldberg remembers her childhood as a happy one, even though her father deserted the family soon after her birth. Her parents never divorced, however, and Goldberg never learned why they broke up in the first place. According to her, Emma Johnson has always been "pretty closemouthed" about that particular subject. Goldberg went through childhood without knowing her father, although she did make her peace with him in later years.

Emma Johnson, on the other hand, was always there. She raised her two children, Caryn and Clyde, with a firm hand, determined to see them grow up with definite values and ideals. Goldberg believes that had her mother been born at a later time, she could have become a doctor. That had been one of Emma Johnson's dreams, but she had never had the opportunity to fulfill it. Instead, she supported her family as a practical nurse and later as a Head Start teacher. Without question, she was the most influential person in her young daughter's life.

"My mother's great," Goldberg later declared. "She has the major looks. She could stop you from doing anything, through a closed door even, with a single look . . . that death-ray look that could melt concrete. Without saying a word, she just has that power to, you know, rip out your tonsils."

Because Clyde was older than Caryn by six years, the two were not always close. Clyde always seemed to be out playing softball. But there was plenty of affection in the Johnson home, and there was always enough food on the table. The brother-sister relationship became strained when Clyde grew up and moved to Alabama, but some years later, Goldberg made an effort to reunite the family. And with the exception of her father, she succeeded.

Goldberg remembers her childhood as nonracist. "Chelsea was a neighborhood full of blacks, whites, Greeks, Jews, Puerto Ricans, and Italians. You had to speak a smattering of all the languages because you had to be able to ask if your friend was home and if you could stay for dinner." The experience stayed with her. "I don't think of things in terms of color," she recently said. "Hollywood does. When I grew up, color was never an issue. My mother would say, 'Look, you're black. You woke up black this morning, you'll go to bed black tonight. But it doesn't make any difference.' "

The world being what it is, it sometimes made a difference to other people. As a teenager, Goldberg occasionally dated white boys. "Why should I be worried about whether or not a guy's white?" she recently asserted. "If he's an ax murderer, then I'm concerned." People in her Chelsea neighborhood did not always share this view. Goldberg remembers walking with a white date and getting pelted with eggs.

"I remember being comfortable and confident when I was a child," Goldberg said in a personal interview. "All our holidays were filled with cheer." As a youngster, she was encouraged by her mother to take advantage of what New York City had to offer. And there was a good deal to see. She took buses to watch Leonard Bernstein conduct young people's concerts. She went to the museums, to the Hayden Planetarium, and to Coney Island. Every day there was something new to investigate. Be curious, her

With the Capitol as a backdrop, young Americans protest U.S. involvement in the Vietnam War during a 1969 demonstration in Washington, D.C. Goldberg and many others who grew up during this era retained the belief that they had the power to change the world.

mother advised, ask questions. Goldberg took that advice and is still taking it.

Although she now spends a great deal of her time in California, Goldberg speaks of her native city with nostalgia. As a child, she felt that she was growing up in a magic kingdom—ice skating in Central Park and watching the Macy's Thanksgiving Day parade every year. "Kids had hope growing up in the 1960s," she reflected.

Indeed, during the 1960s, American society did appear to be poised on the brink of some fundamental change. There was electricity in the air, and the decade was marked by turbulence, great events, and some memorable personalities.

The 1960s were also a time of violence, frantic change, and tragedy. Shortly after the youthful and dashing John F. Kennedy became the 35th president of the United States, he engaged in a test of wills with Nikita Khrushchev, the leader of the Soviet Union. The Soviets had placed nuclear missiles on the island of Cuba, 90 miles from the shores of the United States, and Kennedy demanded that Khrushchev remove the missiles at once. The armed forces of both superpowers were on the alert, and nuclear war seemed only hours away, when the Russian leader backed down and took the missiles out of Cuba.

A genuine tragedy did strike a year later, on November 22, 1963, when Kennedy was assassinated in Dallas, Texas. Five years later, his younger brother Robert was assassinated in Los Angeles while campaigning for the presidency. In the years between these two terrible events, American society became increasingly divided over the growing U.S. involvement in the Asian country of Vietnam and increasingly hostile over the issue of civil rights for black Americans. Demonstrations and sit-ins were often marked by violence.

The fight for civil rights in particular was a long and difficult one. In the end, the cause of equal justice prevailed when the Civil Rights Bill was passed in 1964. The bill banned racial discrimination in schools, voting places, public facilities, and government programs. It said that all Americans, regardless of their skin color, would be treated equally under the law. But the cost of this great achievement was high, because the resentment aroused by the long civil rights campaign lingered on. Two months before Robert Kennedy's death, the leader of the civil rights movement, Martin Luther King, Jr., was struck down by an assassin's bullet as he stood on a motel balcony in Memphis, Tennessee. Thus, the nation lost three of its greatest young leaders during one turbulent decade.

The 1960s ended with a spectacular event. On July 28, 1969, American astronaut Neil A. Armstrong became the first human being in history to step on the moon. With perhaps 1 billion people watching on television, the blurry figure in his bulky space suit carefully lifted one foot from the landing pad of the *Eagle* spacecraft and set it down on the Sea of Tranquility. "That's one small step for man," said Armstrong, "and one giant leap for mankind."

All decades throughout history have had their share of dazzling personalities in addition to their more sober political figures. The 1960s were no exception. A young model from England shocked the fashion world, not merely because of the miniskirts she wore but also because it was difficult to see her if she stood sideways. Appropriately, she was known as Twiggy. Hollywood's most glamorous and beautiful star, Elizabeth Taylor, kept the gossip columns busy with her romance with and eventual marriage (and remarriage) to the British actor Richard Burton. Jackie Kennedy, wife of the late president, shocked many Americans when she married the Greek shipping tycoon Aristotle Onassis. The handsome and flamboyant Cassius Clay, later known as Muhammad Ali, turned the boxing world upside down by boasting about his abilities in the ring and then making his boasts stand up. The face of popular music changed forever when an unscrubbed 22-year-old named Bob Dylan walked onstage with his guitar in 1963 and sang a song called "Blowin' in the Wind," a sweeping condemnation of the political system. But of all the figures who came and went during the decade, none had such a powerful effect on all age groups as four young men with pudding-bowl haircuts and odd-looking suits who produced a musical sound unlike any heard before. George, Paul, Ringo, and John—the Beatles, from Liverpool, England—not only changed the public's listening habits but also began a revolution in style.

Although most black teenagers at the time were enthralled by the Motown sound, featuring such stars as the Supremes, Martha and the Vandellas, and Marvin Gaye, Goldberg was a Beatles fan. When asked about this in a 1994 magazine interview, she responded, "It's just . . . they were different. They weren't like anybody else. And I've always been kind of fascinated by the unusual. Because I was kind of different, but I couldn't prove it. But I *knew*—I knew I wasn't like everybody else. So it just sort of grabbed my heart somewhere."

As Goldberg has claimed, the 1960s were, above all, years of hope for young people. They believed that despite all the obstacles, changes were, in Bob Dylan's words, "blowin' in the wind." Even after the deaths of King and the Kennedys, they believed that the evils behind these events could be dealt with and that they would be the ones to fix things. And so they marched on Washington and sat in at segregated lunch counters in the South and put flowers in their

The Beatles wave to London fans before embarking on a tour of the United States in August 1964. Though most black American teenagers were caught up in the Motown phenomenon, Goldberg adored the trendsetting British rockers: "They weren't like anybody else," she recalled.

New York youngsters present The Pied Piper of Hamlin *at the Helena Rubinstein Performing Arts Workshops, where Goldberg got her start at the age of eight. "I always knew I'd be a performer," she later said.*

hair and said that love could save the world. To most Americans of older generations, the children of the 1960s were simply bizarre. People called them hippies and flower children and wondered why they refused to be like their parents.

Although Caryn Johnson was still a bit young to become a true part of the hippie culture, its atmosphere surrounded her and many of its values became hers. She later said about herself, "I was born a hippie and will be till I die. When I say hippie, I

mean humanist. Environmentalist. Someone who wants world peace. Zen politics. Sunshine, rainbows, God." Perhaps the "do-your-own-thing" attitude of the times, combined with the big-city flavor of the Chelsea neighborhood, caused Caryn to feel older than her years. Yet her mother's values remained part of her also.

For Emma Johnson, the hippie concept of "dropping out" was definitely not "in." Instead, she told her daughter that hard work was the only way to get what she wanted in life. "If you're not willing to do that, then you're probably not going to get it," Emma Johnson insisted. She gave Caryn and Clyde an idea of what life could and should be and how they could take part in it. "It was never intimated to me that I couldn't be exactly what I wanted to be," Goldberg later recalled.

As she grew up, there was no doubt in her mind that she wanted to be a performer. She had always known that. Even when she was very young, she watched a lot of movies, both in movie theaters and on television. Sometimes she would watch three or four movies a day. The films she loved best were from the 1930s, 1940s, and 1950s. Among her favorite stars were John Garfield, Joan Crawford, and Carole Lombard.

She learned from all of them. "When I was a kid," she later recalled, "you could watch a Carole Lombard film and a John Garfield film and a Bette Davis film and a Henry Fonda film, and they'd all play the same emotion completely differently. So during the course of a day, you would learn four or five ways to do any one thing. Today, I use the same technique; watch, absorb, and then give it back."

To Caryn, acting just seemed a natural thing to do. At the age of eight, she had asked her mother if it was possible to be a princess. Emma Johnson replied that when a person is acting, he or she can be anything. Caryn replied, "Well, then, I'm getting into this!" She began acting with the Helena Rubinstein Performing Arts Workshops. She performed at the Hudson Guild, a neighborhood settlement house, which is still very much a part of the Chelsea scene.

Caryn's love of the theater immediately communicated itself to others. Sister Jeanne Fielder, her seventh- and eighth-grade teacher at a local Catholic school, St. Columba, recently said in an interview, "The Hudson Guild was Caryn's first love. Acting was in her genes. She was a performer. You couldn't miss it. She had the lead in several plays; she played the lead in every play she was in. She was Maria in the *Sound of Music*, as I recall. The Hudson Guild was really Caryn's first love."

Sister Jeanne Fielder still teaches New York youngsters, now at St. Jean Baptiste. When asked what kind of student Caryn was, she replied, "Delightful! She was full of the devil, an average student, and very popular with her classmates. She would pull a prank and look at you with those great big eyes, and you couldn't stay mad. She smiled at you so innocently that you just melted."

The school principal at the time, Sister Marie Cafferty, remembers Caryn as "frisky, friendly, outgoing, and full of fun. Caryn was in many ways a typical eighth grader. But she was the center of attention when she walked into a group. Our school was racially mixed and she got along with everyone."

It would seem, then, that Caryn Johnson's future was essentially charted back in her grade-school years. Without a doubt, she was going to be a performer. But turning that big smile at St. Columba's into a wide grin on the television screen called for a great deal of effort. The journey from Chelsea, New York City, to Hollywood, California, would be a rocky one indeed. ❖

3

OUT OF THE RAIN

ONE OF THE many contradictions about the teenage years is that young people often see themselves far differently than they are seen by others. Caryn Johnson was, in that respect, a typical teenager. She recently said in a personal interview, "I was always different. My likes and dislikes were different than the crowd's." She insisted that all through school she was unpopular. Her teachers and a family friend have different recollections.

Don Sledge, a longtime family friend who has worked at the Hudson Guild since the days when Goldberg began performing there, claims that she was always very popular. "She was funny, and when you're funny, kids like you. She was an outgoing kid, always talented. She seemed cut out to be an actress or comedian even then. And she was determined. You just knew that. She had a goal. Never shy. She wasn't ashamed to ask anything she needed to know. I remember one time that a neighborhood program was in trouble. It was directed by Frank Strock. He ran a program to involve and help young people, sort of a community teen counsel. Well, the funds ran out and his job and the whole program were in danger. So, Caryn took over. She ran right out in the street, yelling and performing. She even started pulling out water hoses, anything to get anyone's attention. She

Goldberg in the early days of her professional career. An energetic, upbeat teenager with a natural curiosity about the world, Goldberg had to struggle with a learning disability, a drug problem, and a failed marriage before she could devote herself to acting.

Antidrug demonstrators march along New York's Sixth Avenue in 1970. After overcoming her own dependence on marijuana and LSD in the late 1960s, Goldberg has repeatedly warned young people about the dangers of drug use.

wanted to get the neighborhood people and politicians to hear the problem. And she did."

Life in the early 1960s did not seem all that bad for this young black American living in Chelsea. She had a caring, if firm, mother; an easygoing, if distant, brother; a secure, if fatherless, home; and an enormous, if yet untried, talent. But things are rarely what they seem to be.

Caryn Johnson graduated from St. Columba in 1969 and entered New York City's Washington Irving High School in the fall. She never finished. Her road took a detour and she dropped out—out of school, her neighborhood, her old life.

"I couldn't understand what they were doing there," she later said of her decision to leave school. One reason for her problems with school went undetected at the time, as in the case of many other students of that era. She suffers from dyslexia. Dyslexia is a not-uncommon reading disorder that causes a person to see letters in reverse order. If recognized early, it can be handled fairly well. Goldberg says of her problem, "I learned how to deal with dyslexia through a lot of hard work and the help of a lot of different people. If someone feels they have a problem with reading or learning, they should make someone aware of it. There's so much more knowledge about dyslexia now and they could get the help they need."

However, the main reason Goldberg dropped out was her involvement with marijuana and LSD, the fashionable drugs of the 1960s. Perhaps it was her restless nature and endless curiosity that led her to experiment with drugs, something she is firmly against today. Looking back, she says it was easy to experiment in the 1960s; everyone seemed to be doing it, and no one seemed to be talking about the terrible consequences. Whatever the real reasons for her drug use, Goldberg has basically kept them to herself. For all her outspokenness and her desire to communicate with the public as a performer, Goldberg has always been a very private person. As Don Sledge recalls, "She kept her business to herself. What she couldn't hide, she couldn't. But she tried to keep her private business out of sight."

Sledge also remembers Goldberg's early teenage years as a time of trouble. "The drug problem hit. Emma [Johnson] wouldn't speak of it. Caryn just dropped out of sight. She was heard of from time to time, but she was gone from the community."

Sometimes when a youngster becomes involved with drugs, the blame falls on the parents. In her own case, Goldberg has refused to go along with this. "My mother was not a drug addict and not on welfare," she stated. "You become a teenager and nobody can tell you anything." Goldberg speaks of the 1960s as a "time when you could use the stuff and walk down the street. You were high, everybody was. We could sleep in Central Park. It was a time of drugs and powders. That's when I used drugs. People seem to want me to have come from the dregs and dragged myself up, but that's just not the way it was."

However it was, Goldberg was headed for trouble. At some point, she knew that she had to decide what she really wanted. She says that her drug problem probably began to end when she got bored with it. "There ain't no joy in a high—*none*," she stated in a 1991 magazine interview. "You *think* there's a joy in a high because it feels good temporarily. But it feels good less and less often, so you've got to do it more and more often. It ain't your friend. . . . I tell kids, 'Save the money and just kill yourself because [if you're using drugs] that's what you're doing.' "

At the age of 17, Caryn checked into Horizon House, a drug treatment program in New York City. She stayed with the treatment and got herself together. People in the community knew when the drug scene was over for her. "She left as Caryn," says Don Sledge, "and came back as Whoopi." He added that she was still the same person underneath, "but mature, confident. She knew the ropes now. She knew what she wanted. She always knew where she wanted to go. She just had problems along the way. But she got there. Kept her eye on the road and did what she said she would do. And she never forgot her friends, her past, those who helped her along the way."

Goldberg still visits Don Sledge and the sisters from St. Columba whenever she is back in New York and has some free time. "I defy anybody to say she isn't loyal," says Sledge. "To know her is to love her. Believe it."

Sledge punctuates his contention that Goldberg remembers her friends by telling of a surprise visit to the Hudson Guild one rainy night. Goldberg's brother, Clyde, dropped in first. "He chatted, said he was in town for a while, was real casual. The event that night was a Hudson Guild party for Vista [a government-sponsored organization that benefits the poor]. After we talked a bit, I realized that Clyde had carried two umbrellas in with him and had placed them on the windowsill. I asked him about that, but he just played dumb. Then, wearing a big smile and calling 'Surprise!' the owner of the second umbrella walked in. Sure enough, Whoopi had come in out of the rain."

Although Goldberg had conquered her drug habit, by the age of 18 she was enmeshed in another difficult situation—but not with drugs. After dating her counselor at Horizon House for a time, she wound up married to him. "It seemed like the thing to do," she said. But the marriage lasted only two years. "It wasn't for me," Goldberg reflected. "You get married because you love someone and for no other reason. It can only last if you're deeply in love, and we weren't."

The marriage did last long enough, however, for Goldberg to give birth to her only child, Alexandrea—named for Alexander the Great, one of history's most renowned conquerors. After her divorce, Goldberg lost touch with Alexandrea's father, and there was no further contact between them.

For a short time, Goldberg—divorced before the age of 20—moved back to her mother's house with Alexandrea. Then came a phone call from a friend who was heading for California and asked if Goldberg wanted to come along. She certainly did.

In 1974, with her young daughter in tow, Goldberg headed for California "in a barf-green car via Lubbock, Texas." She imagined they were going to Hollywood and was appalled when her friend landed them in San Diego. But Goldberg was in California, 3,000 miles closer to the stardom she envisioned. "Acting is the one thing I always knew I could do," she recalled. A more immediate concern, however, was eating—and caring for an infant. ✺

4

"I EARNED THIS"

❧

DESPITE HER TALENT and her never-say-die attitude, the future did not look bright for Whoopi Goldberg in 1974. She was a single mother, a former drug user, and a high school dropout. She was in a strange city with few friends and no money. Her next move was by no means clear.

Since it did not appear that anyone was going to offer her a dressing room with a star on it, Goldberg went looking for a job. She got her license as a beautician and ended up fixing hair in a funeral parlor. She later said it was not a bad job because the surroundings were quiet and none of the customers complained about her work. She also worked as a bank teller and a bricklayer, and she took a couple of construction jobs that involved putting in plasterboard. But performing was always on her mind. She finally became involved with the San Diego Repertory Theater, getting small parts in a number of plays and developing her versatility. She once played five characters in the Charles Dickens classic *A Christmas Carol*. She also did a few routines as a fast-talking stand-up comedian. Eventually, she met a fellow actor named Don Victor and agreed to work as his partner. Together, Goldberg and Victor did some late-night theater routines around town.

An exuberant Whoopi Goldberg, photographed in 1984, when her comedic talents were beginning to shine on Broadway. Before reaching this plateau, Goldberg endured 10 years of hard work and poverty, including a stint on welfare.

The San Diego Repertory was keeping Goldberg busy, but it was not paying her bills. Finally, a friend suggested that Goldberg should consider going on welfare. After all, there was Alexandrea to think of. Goldberg did eventually accept public assistance, and she remained on the welfare rolls for the next several years. She recalls, "I wasn't raised in a welfare household, so this was a tough thing to do." But she also says, "I'm glad they were there, although it's a system I've come to see, in hindsight, that's devised for you not to get off."

Years later, some of her worst experiences as a welfare recipient were fresh in Goldberg's mind. "The welfare workers used to make these surprise visits," she said in a 1991 interview, "because you weren't allowed to have friends—especially not friends to whom you might want to be polite and *feed* something. If a welfare worker did surprise you and you happened to have a friend in the house with a plate of food in front of them, it would be deducted from your money the next month." She went on to say that nothing in her life had given her more pleasure than reaching the point when she could support herself again: "The *greatest* thing I ever was able to do was give a welfare check back. I brought it back to the welfare department and said, 'Here, I don't need this anymore.' "

Before that could happen, Goldberg had a long road to travel. Her first break came in 1980 when she and Victor were invited to Berkeley, California, to perform some of their material. Victor became ill and was unable to go. Goldberg decided to take a gamble. She took Alexandrea and moved north to Berkeley, joining a well-known local troupe called the Blake Street Hawkeyes. It was there that she created and began to develop *The Spook Show*, in which she portrayed a variety of offbeat characters. To her own amazement, the first time she unveiled *The Spook*

Goldberg appears in a 1981 production of Bertolt Brecht's Mother Courage *at the San Diego Repertory Theater. Working in repertory, where a group of actors play different parts in a series of productions, helped Goldberg expand her range and versatility.*

Show, the audience went wild. This was the beginning of her career as a solo artist.

The Blake Street Hawkeyes eventually went on to a successful season in San Francisco. Following this, they toured the United States and Europe. In 1983, the troupe settled in for an extended run in New York at the Dance Theater Workshop. Goldberg's *Spook Show* routine was now highly developed and an important part of the Blake Street presentation.

Each night in *The Spook Show*, Goldberg created an array of characters (whom she called spooks) that she continued to develop and redefine with each performance, depending on her mood and that of the audience. She did not use makeup or change costumes when she turned into another character, but the differences between the characters were so sharp that the viewer might well have thought that more than one performer was onstage.

Four particular characters dominated the performance, drawing howls of laughter from the audience. At the same time, though, Goldberg's "spooks" conveyed the pain and heartache suffered by many people in modern society.

There is the white, California-based "surfer chick" popularly known as a valley girl. She talks like an airhead and lives for the shopping mall. However, the comedy turns to pathos when the valley girl finds that she is pregnant; frightened and not knowing where to turn for help, she tries to perform an abortion on herself.

The second character is Fontaine, a jive-talking, bigmouthed former drug addict who has a Ph.D. in literature. In one of his monologues, Fontaine discusses his humorous experiences on an airplane while traveling to Amsterdam, Holland. Then he cuts the comedy and, still in character, begins to talk about visiting the museum honoring Anne Frank, the young Jewish girl who, with her family, hid from German forces in Amsterdam for two years during World War II. Eventually, the family was discovered, and young Anne died in a concentration camp. Badman Fontaine becomes thoroughly shaken as he tells his story, and so does the audience.

Another character is a physically disabled young woman who is getting married in two weeks. Goldberg recognized that people were uncomfortable at first with this character, because they thought she was going to make fun of a disability. Instead, Goldberg says, what her character does is talk to people as a human being, and pretty soon they forget all about the so-called handicap.

The fourth main *Spook Show* character, and perhaps the most endearing and sad, is the nine-year-old black girl who traipses across the stage with a light-colored shirt draped across her forehead and hanging down her back. "My long blonde tresses," she says sweetly. Then she explains that she does not want to be black anymore. Instead, she wants white skin, blue eyes, and long blonde hair. Why? Because when she grows up, she wants to go on "The Love Boat," and everybody on "The Love Boat" has long blonde tresses.

Goldberg explained that she never really worked on these characters, as other comedians do. They just seemed to live within her, saying things she would never say. Whenever Goldberg did *The Spook Show*, she disappeared, and the characters took over. She also pointed out that although the character Fontaine may make drugs look very hip, she has been careful to keep any drug use out of her films. That is because she is so adamantly against drugs, and she is very conscious of any possible influence she may have on young people.

One night during her run at the Dance Theater Workshop, the well-known producer and director Mike Nichols caught Goldberg's act. He was astonished and moved, and he immediately went to see Goldberg backstage. He told her he would like to produce *The Spook Show* on Broadway. Goldberg recalled that her answer was a simple one: "Yes! Yes!"

The Spook Show became a smash hit at the Lyceum Theater, only a mile or so from Goldberg's old neighborhood. Renamed *Whoopi Goldberg: Direct from Broadway,* the show was taped and shown on cable television. In 1985, the record album of the Broadway show won the Grammy Award for the best comedy recording. One thing often leads to another. One night, the film director Steven Spielberg happened to be in New York, and he went to see Goldberg's Broadway show. At that time Spielberg— whose credits include *Jaws, Jurassic Park,* and the Oscar-winning *Schindler's List*—was casting parts for *The Color Purple.* Based on a highly acclaimed novel by Alice Walker, *The Color Purple* tells the story of a 14-year-old southern black girl named Celie, uneducated and abused, who finds the courage to live and to love.

The Color Purple is certainly no comedy. But Spielberg, like many outstanding directors, had an instinct for finding the right person to fill a crucial role. After watching the gifted young comedian on the stage, he decided that Goldberg would be perfect for the serious role of Celie.

Goldberg had never made a movie, so Spielberg appeared to be taking a wild gamble. But the results proved that he knew exactly what he was doing. *The Color Purple* was a hit with the critics and a blockbuster at the box office, and much of the film's success had to do with Goldberg's performance. Film critic Steve Erickson, writing in *Rolling Stone,* described the effect of Goldberg's talent:

She says everything with her face, and her voice: not the words of the voice but its sound, and the mouth that speaks it. The mouth looks to be from somewhere other than her face, as though it arrived later and decided this was a face, after all, that would never upstage it. . . . [The scene] might never have worked at all but for that face and that voice. In the juke joint, singer Shug [played by Margaret Avery] sings to Celie, the story's much-abused central character. In the picture's single best bit of acting, Goldberg simply watches Shug, one emotion after another bubbling to the surface of that face, each bursting the emotion that came before and then wanting to be contradicted by the next.

Many other critics and film industry professionals were equally impressed with Goldberg's performance as Celie. Rarely does a performer's first film venture result in an Academy Award nomination, but in 1985, Golberg was nominated for Best Performance by an Actress in a Leading Role. Although the award that year went to the veteran actress Geraldine Page for her work in *The Trip to Bountiful*, Goldberg had unquestionably become a Hollywood star. Her performance in *The Color Purple* did earn her a Golden Globe Award and the Image Award of the National Association for the Advancement of Colored People (NAACP).

Goldberg made many movies after that initial success, among them *Jumpin' Jack Flash* (1986), *Burglar* (1987), *Clara's Heart* (1988), *The Telephone* (1988), *Ghost* (1990), *The Long Walk Home* (1990), *Soapdish* (1991), *The Player* (1992), *Sister Act* (1992), *Sarafina!* (1992), and *Made in America* (1993). Some of these films, such as *Burglar*, were, she acknowledged, just light-hearted entertainment and fun to do. Some of them, such as *The Player*, directed by Robert Altman, were serious works that drew praise from movie critics.

Even when Goldberg appeared in lesser films, critics often stated that her performance was the best

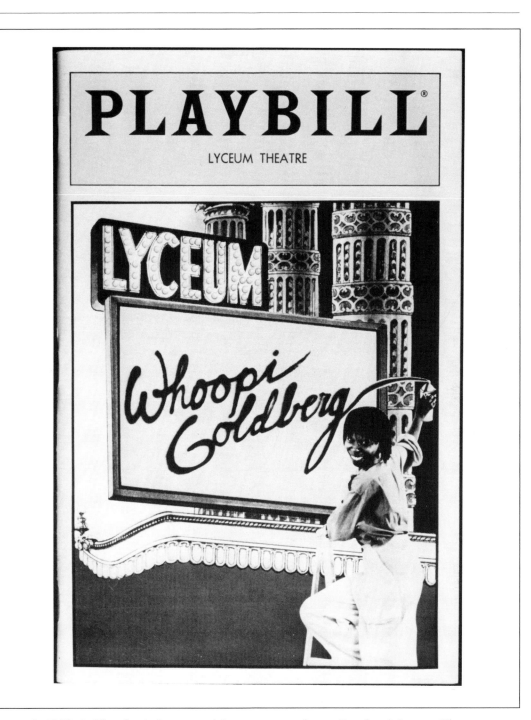

In 1985, Goldberg hit the big time with her one-woman show at Broadway's Lyceum Theatre.

Performing one of the most heart-wrenching segments of her one-woman show, Goldberg portrays a nine-year-old black girl who drapes a shirt over her head and pretends that she has long blonde hair.

thing about the movie. On her own, she could make something out of very little. *Sister Act* is a case in point. This funny but so-so movie turned out to be a "sleeper." This is the name given to a film that is far more popular than expected. Goldberg gave it class—and laughs.

In *Sister Act,* Goldberg plays a character named Deloris Von Cartier, a brassy, second-rate nightclub singer in Reno, Nevada. Quite by accident, Deloris witnesses her mobster boyfriend committing a murder. She quickly realizes that unless she gets out of town quickly, she is going to be the next victim.

With a policeman's help, Deloris is put into the witness protection program and goes undercover. She is sent to a most unlikely spot for a lounge singer, one where the mob would never think of looking for her—a San Francisco convent, where she is disguised as a nun. Deloris is not at all happy with the arrangement, and the mother superior, the only one at the convent who knows her real identity, is aghast.

Not surprisingly, Deloris turns the poor, inner-city convent upside down. The other nuns love her; the mother superior contemplates resigning. As her crowning achievement, Deloris transforms the truly terrible convent choir into a first-rate singing act that even the pope comes to see. In the process, Deloris finds friendship, love, and a sense of self-worth in what was, for her, a most unlikely place.

Sister Act gave Goldberg a chance to display a previously undiscovered talent—singing. She worked with a voice coach every day for about a month before tackling the movie. Though she more than held her own, she remained modest about her vocal ability. "I'm still more comfortable singing in the shower," she insisted later. In the end, *Sister Act* meant more to Goldberg than comedy and singing. She wanted to do the part because she believed it would add another dimension to her already diverse career, and

Goldberg's performance as Celie in the 1985 film The Color Purple *won rave reviews and electrified filmgoers across the nation. Nominated for an Academy Award for Best Actress, Goldberg emerged from her film debut as a full-fledged Hollywood star.*

As Deloris Von Cartier, Goldberg rehearses a choir of nuns in the 1992 hit comedy Sister Act. *The highly successful film marked Goldberg's debut as a singer and also meant a great deal to her personally: "This story is about self-discovery and discovering that when you're open to receiving help, it comes to you," she said.*

in the process, she might learn something: "This story is about self-discovery and discovering that when you're open to receiving help, it comes to you."

After the surprise success of *Sister Act*, which grossed more than $300 million, one reporter quipped: "This is the year that Whoopi Goldberg finally became bigger than her hair." Moviegoers liked *Sister Act* so much that the producers released a sequel, *Sister Act 2: Back in the Habit*, in 1993. At this point, Goldberg was commanding $8 million per

film, making her one of the highest-paid performers in Hollywood.

Next to *The Color Purple*, Goldberg's most highly acclaimed dramatic performance came in *Ghost*, a combination of fantasy, thriller, and romance that costarred Demi Moore and Patrick Swayze. In the film, which is set in New York, Goldberg portrays Oda Mae Brown, a neighborhood fortune-teller. Essentially a fraud who preys on gullible customers, Goldberg's character suddenly finds herself caught up

Goldberg exults after receiving an Academy Award for her performance in Ghost. *Though she had long dreamed of winning an Oscar, the usually talkative Goldberg was tongue-tied at first. "I was so floored," she admitted, "there was nothing I could do except sort of gasp, 'Thank you.' "*

in a genuine mystical experience when she is possessed by the spirit of a man who has been murdered by a crooked business partner. Believing that the partner will now try to harm the girlfriend he left behind, the ghost uses Oda Mae as a go-between to protect his lover. Amazed, and somewhat uncomfortable, to find that she has genuine powers, Oda Mae finally succeeds in her profession.

Goldberg's work in *Ghost* earned her a second Oscar nomination, this time for Best Performance by an Actress in a Supporting Role. Many people had felt that Goldberg was denied an Oscar for *The*

Color Purple because of the controversy surrounding the film—there were complaints that it unfairly portrayed black men as habitual abusers of women—and because of Steven Spielberg's apparent unpopularity among the Hollywood establishment. At the 1991 ceremonies, Goldberg finally received her due as an actress and won the Academy Award. In doing so, she became the first black actress to win an Oscar since Hattie McDaniel was honored in 1939 for her role in *Gone with the Wind*.

Goldberg, who generally favors the casual approach in clothes and appearance, looked unusually regal on Oscar night in a floor-length black sequined gown. Because she had been practicing her acceptance speech from the time she was a little girl in Chelsea, she should not have had much difficulty walking to the stage and receiving her award. But the reality of the event nearly overwhelmed her.

As Goldberg later explained in an interview for *Parade* magazine, "When I finally got the opportunity to give the speech I'd been practicing for years, I didn't have it. I was so floored, there was nothing I could do except sort of gasp, 'Thank you.' I looked around and saw all those people sitting there—Sophia Loren, Gregory Peck. And then I just wanted to say 'thank you' to them for being in all those movies I got to watch. For letting me come and play." When she finally found her voice and gave her acceptance speech, she admitted that she had wanted an Oscar ever since she was a child. "My brother's sitting out there," she told the audience, "saying, 'Thank God, we don't have to listen to her anymore.' "

The Oscar was truly a culmination for Goldberg, who said in a private interview, "I know I always wanted to act. I don't know if that shaped my life or if I shaped my life to make that fit. But I always knew that was what I wanted to do."

Many people, especially young people, dream of making it big in show business. Few of them ever realize their dreams, and few appreciate how much talent, hard work, hardship, and perseverance—mixed with a bit of luck—it takes to get there. Dreams alone never do it. What looks like an "overnight success" generally has years of hard work behind it. In this respect, Goldberg was no different from any other "overnight success" when she thanked the audience for her Oscar. Speaking to reporters after the ceremonies, she was able to say in all honesty, "I earned this."

Winning an Oscar is traditionally the ticket to genuine superstardom, and this certainly proved to be true in Goldberg's case. Bolstered by her new status, she expressed herself not only as a performer but as a person. The public and the press responded. In 1992, Goldberg earned one of *Glamour* magazine's Women of the Year awards for being, in the words of the editors, "the funniest, feistiest actor we know." *Glamour* said:

> No one dominated the entertainment world this year like Whoopi Goldberg. Who will ever forget her as a detective in *The Player?* She showed off the range of her talent in two other films, the inspirational *Sarafina!* and the top-grossing comedy *Sister Act.* She continued her role on *Star Trek: The Next Generation.* She published her first book, a modern fairy tale called *Alice,* and yes, that was her voice on two children's television shows. She also debuted as a late-night talk-show host and served as first female host of the Grammy Awards. She is famous for her independent spirit. Although fiercely proud of her African-American heritage, this mother and recent grandmother refused to vote for *Jungle Fever,* the film of black director Spike Lee, at the Cannes Film Festival, and she defied objections to her making a movie in South Africa. Her chief accomplishment this year, she says, is "staying who I am with very little compromise."

Goldberg also made her presence felt in the political arena. Though her independent views make it hard for people to pin her down as either a liberal or a conservative, she had always spoken out for constructive changes in society and vocally supported the administration of President Bill Clinton. Along with the Olympic track champion Jackie Joyner-Kersee, she was instrumental in setting up a fund to finance female political candidates, for which she was honored by First Lady Hillary Rodham Clinton. Goldberg was also cited in conjunction with University of Oklahoma law professor Anita Hill for "lighting the way to political changes."

Those who knew Caryn Johnson during her Chelsea days, when she was part of a generation that dreamed of changing the world, would have had no trouble recognizing her actions as Whoopi Goldberg. ❧

5

BRANCHING OUT

W ITH HER OSCAR securely tucked under her arm, Goldberg marched off into the glamorous world of Hollywood success. Her credits kept on rolling. She seemed to be everywhere—on stage, screen, television. But it was not always easy.

"People think I get tons of scripts," Goldberg reflected. "But I don't. Nobody can write for me. Writing for Whoopi Goldberg is a little like spitting in a high wind. I just take the best of what I'm offered, and that's all you can do."

With all this fame, of course, came material success. Goldberg's life in the 1990s was a far cry from her existence as a welfare mother. In addition to her home outside Los Angeles, she had a farm in New England where she kept three horses with names that sound as though they came from a childhood dream—Peppy Bell, Shadow, and Quisma. For Goldberg, the farm became a place where she could retreat from the world and just be Caryn Johnson. But this did not happen often.

"Sometimes fame is fun," Goldberg confessed. She also admitted that it was not always fun for her family. Both her mother and brother moved to California to be near her, settling in the San Francisco Bay area. Goldberg has always maintained close ties with them, and they have reveled in her success. But

Goldberg and her daughter, Alexandrea, attend the 1991 Academy Awards. Though Goldberg felt that she had made many mistakes as a parent— "I wasn't a mommy-type person," she once admitted— she was highly supportive when Alexandrea needed her most.

the strains of stardom have taken the greatest toll on Goldberg's daughter, Alexandrea.

One of the most difficult episodes in the mother-daughter relationship began when Goldberg learned that Alexandrea was pregnant at the age of 15. "You go around telling kids about what's right to do, and your own daughter does not follow your advice," she lamented. Although Goldberg was not happy with the news, she supported Alexandrea's decision to have the child. "I figured if she was old enough to make that decision, I had better be there for her," she said. In a magazine interview, she made a point about reproductive freedom for women: "I'm glad . . . that this baby was a choice and not a forced issue—that she could have decided not to carry it had she wanted that. That's very important to me—that she made the choice herself."

When Alexandrea had her baby, Amarah Skye, in 1989, both she and Goldberg came in for public criticism. Goldberg received a number of angry letters condemning both her own attitude and her daughter's action. She was both amused and annoyed by the implication that her money and fame should have prevented her or her daughter from having a problem that so many other families have shared. But she also owned up to her own shortcomings as a parent.

"I wasn't a mommy-type person," she said. "I'm a great pal. But now I believe you can't just be a friend to your kid. You've got to make the decisions; you have to be the person in charge. In my attempt to be what my mother wasn't—which was flexible—I might have been too much of a pal."

Alexandrea and Amarah Skye live near Goldberg, and their relationship is a close one. Goldberg has said that her granddaughter is one of the delights of her life.

Following the publication of her children's book Alice, *Goldberg appears with actor LeVar Burton on the educational TV show "Reading Rainbow."* Goldberg's *first venture as an author was rated "smart and strong" by the New York Times.*

Amarah Skye may have been inspiration for Goldberg's first venture into literature. In September 1991, Bantam Books announced the publication of *Alice,* a children's story by Whoopi Goldberg. Goldberg wrote the book, she said, because she "wanted to give kids a modern fairy tale they could relate to that had a black kid in it."

Goldberg's original and outrageous fairy tale, illustrated by John Rocco, concerns an Alice whose adventures are not in Wonderland, like Lewis Carroll's Alice, but in New Jersey. Alice is a very single-minded young woman. She wants to get rich. She feels that her present life is not bad. But if she were rich, she would *really* be happy.

Alice enters every contest, sweepstakes, and raffle she hears about. One day the mail carrier brings her a mysterious message—a sweepstakes ticket that may change her life. But there is a catch. Alice must travel to New York City to claim her prize.

Alice sets off for the big city with her two best friends: Robin, who lives next door and does bad card tricks, and a "sort of" invisible Italian rabbit named Sal. Fascinating, madcap adventures follow as Alice races the clock to claim her prize before the deadline, contending with a host of urban characters who seem bent on spoiling her chance at a fortune.

Despite its modern setting, the story is, after all, a fairy tale, and like all fairy tales it has a moral. By the story's end, young Alice has learned some valuable lessons about herself and about the value of friendship.

According to a reviewer in the *New York Times*, Goldberg succeeded at creating a first-rate children's story. "The narrative is smart and strong, and Alice is just the kind of urban heroine many of us have been looking for in a children's book: brave but not foolish, loyal and generous, absolutely single-minded, and very funny indeed."

In addition to acting and writing, Goldberg's creative energies took her in other directions, such as television. In 1986, she received a Prime-Time Emmy Award nomination for Best Guest Performer in a Dramatic Series for "Moonlighting," the popular series starring Cybill Shepherd and Bruce Willis. She also starred with Jean Stapleton in "Bagdad Cafe" and made a guest appearance on "A Different World." In 1988, she was nominated for the American Comedy Award for the Funniest Female Performer in a TV Special, "Carol, Carl, Whoopi and Robin," in which she starred along with Carol Burnett, Carl Reiner, and Robin Williams. She also received an Ace Award nomination for HBO's "Whoopi Goldberg's Fontaine

Goldberg appears in the CBS Schoolbreak Special "My Past Is My Own" in 1988. Following her success in The Color Purple, *Goldberg began to make numerous TV appearances, winning a coveted Emmy Award for a guest appearance on "Moonlighting."*

. . . Why Am I Straight?" In 1989 she was one of the nominees for Best Performer in a Children's Special, "My Past Is My Own." In 1992, she received an Emmy as Outstanding Actress in a Drama Series, Television Movie or Mini-Series for her performance as Guinan on "Star Trek: The Next Generation." Along with Billy Crystal and Robin Williams, she won cable TV's Ace Award for "Comic Relief V," an annual special that benefits the homeless.

If anything more were needed to confirm Goldberg's status as a figure on the American scene, she was interviewed on the popular Sunday night TV show "60 Minutes" on February 14, 1993. The inter-

Goldberg shares a laugh with Vice-President Al Gore on her late-night TV talk show, which aired during 1993. Following an unusual format, Goldberg spent each half-hour telecast with a single guest, chatting informally about a wide variety of issues.

viewer was the veteran reporter Ed Bradley, who looked as though he had a hard time keeping a straight face.

The segment of the program that featured Goldberg began with a picture of an old farmhouse in New England. Bradley told the viewers that it was there, miles from nowhere and 3,000 miles from the glamorous world of movie stars, that Goldberg really felt at home. To which Goldberg replied with a grand

smile, "This is how Carole Lombard lived in the movies." She added, "This is me."

Goldberg took Bradley and the TV audience on a tour of the lovely old farmhouse, explaining that she could wind up most everything in the house because the electricity goes out a lot in the country. Though there were paintings by Picasso and other famous artists on the walls, next to her bed Goldberg had "Wise butter popcorn, a Fun Saver flash camera,

Goldberg attends the premiere of the 1993 film Made in America *with costar Ted Danson (right) and supporting actors Will Smith and Nia Long.*

and really weird jelly candies that I like." It was hard to imagine the glamorous Lombard showing off such items in her bedroom.

Also in 1993, Goldberg decided to stretch her career a little further. She switched places with those who had interviewed her over the past few years and became the star of her own half-hour late-night TV talk show. " 'The Whoopi Goldberg Show' was not a show about newsmakers," she later said. "It's about conversing." That was exactly what she did with her guests, conducting the show in a low-key, informal manner. Flashing her toothy, million-dollar smile, one leg tucked up under her on an oversize sofa, she was down-to-earth and friendly, a welcoming host who got people to talk.

Some viewers were disappointed to find Goldberg taking such a relaxed approach. They had tuned in expecting a full dose of her street-smart, feisty, wise-cracking persona. Instead, they saw a soft-spoken, agreeable, almost restrained host. One critic called the show a "slightly off-kilter alternative to the big three—David Letterman, Jay Leno, and Arsenio Hall." Goldberg might talk to Vice-President Al Gore one night and to the rapper Ice T the next. There was no studio audience, no band, no an-nouncer, and only one guest per show. The set was described as dark and "zenlike" (a reference to the meditative mood of Zen Buddhism). Whoever the guest might be, the conversation never got biting or confrontational. "I wanted to make it as comfortable as possible," Goldberg said.

Although "The Whoopi Goldberg Show" is no longer in production, Goldberg was unfazed. Clearly, it was not something in which she had invested her hopes for the future. In fact, the *New York Times* had observed in a review that "[Goldberg] acts as though the show were just something else to do between projects. Some people garden. Whoopi Goldberg does a talk show."

Whatever the critics said, whatever the ratings, Goldberg's guests always seemed to respond to her. Perhaps the relaxed atmosphere that disturbed the critics was just right for the celebrities. For example, during an interview with Alexander Haig, a former secretary of state in the Reagan administration and a

Goldberg enjoys a night out with her second husband, David Claessen, in September 1986. After marrying the Dutch-born cameraman, Goldberg shrugged off criticism from the black community. "Why should I be worried about whether or not a guy's white?" she mused. "If he's an ax murderer, then I'm concerned."

retired military officer, Goldberg wanted to know if she should address him as "General." Haig replied, "Just call me Big Al."

Goldberg also had such guests as Elizabeth Taylor, Elton John, Ted Danson, and Robin Williams. The Temptations dropped by once to perform some of their hits. Track star Carl Lewis chatted about the public's changing view of the Olympic Games. Ed Bradley, who had interviewed Goldberg on "60 Minutes," talked about complaints that the media is too liberal. Rap star L. L. Cool J told Goldberg about his tour to Africa's Ivory Coast.

When asked, Goldberg admitted that the talk-show stint was probably not a great career move. She said she should have been concentrating more on films. But hosting the show was an expression of her intellectual curiosity. In addition to being an avid reader, she likes to find out what is on people's minds. Interviewing them in front of a camera was one way of doing that.

With the talk show out of the way, Goldberg was free to concentrate on acting again. In addition to finding challenging roles, she was determined to change the way people look at actors and acting. Like many other black and ethnic actors, she has constantly come up against stereotyping on the part of casting directors. She never forgot auditioning for a play about Eleanor of Aquitaine, the wife of Louis VII of France and Henry II of England, and being told, "No, you can't play Eleanor of Aquitaine."

"Why not?" Goldberg asked.

"You're black," she was told.

"So what?" she said.

"But she was white," came the reply.

"But this is the theater, honey," Goldberg protested. "This is make-believe. This is not real." The casting director was not convinced.

The situation was no better in the film industry. "I've been told I'm not right for the part because the girl is supposed to be from the Midwest," Goldberg recalled. "Like there was no black people in the Midwest, you know."

Richard Benjamin, a veteran actor who directed the successful 1993 film *Made in America*, starring Goldberg and Ted Danson, understood Goldberg's feelings about films and race. Her arguments caused him to broaden his thinking. *Made in America*, a romantic comedy, concerns Sarah (Goldberg), an African-American bookstore owner whose 17-year-old daughter discovers her father is not dead, as she had always been told. Instead, he turns out to be a loudmouthed car salesman named Hal (played by Danson). In the course of the movie, these incongruous people decide how to handle the situation. Originally, the man and woman in the script were both white, but Benjamin decided that Goldberg could add an extra dimension to the story.

On the whole, Goldberg does not believe that being black has been either a help or a hindrance to her career. "I never think about it," she has said.

Nevertheless, when Goldberg began dating Danson off camera, she added a real-life dimension to the story. During the late 1980s, she had been briefly married to a Dutch-born cameraman named David Claessen. Because both Danson and Claessen were white, Goldberg came in for criticism from both blacks and whites. She did not take it kindly. "I don't even listen," she told *Ebony* magazine. "If I'm looking to make peace in the world, then why do you want to mess with me and tell me I've done the wrong thing? Because [you think] I've let go of my culture? *I'm here.* I don't change my skin every day. Every day I'm out there, every movie I make I'm Black. Every diamond I wear is worn on a Black hand. Of course, nobody has asked me about my first husband [who is Black] because nobody wants to know about that."

Despite high praise for her acting and comedic talents, Goldberg has also been called difficult to work with. Goldberg's response to the charge is brief: "I am." She has never made any attempt to soften her rather colorful language, no matter whom she is with, and she has always been accustomed to saying what is on her mind, on the set and elsewhere. She has been especially vocal when she is on schedule and ready to do her job and others are not equally prepared. "I've worked with some of the best and I know how it's supposed to be," she has said. "But when you're with people who should know better . . . I don't like it, and I don't stand for it. . . . You're not supposed to do that [tell people off], apparently, but I don't know any other way to say I'm distressed."

Ted Danson defended Goldberg against her critics in the following terms: "What she does is disturb the status quo. That's her job." ◕

6
COMIC RELIEF

WHEN GOLDBERG WAS asked, during a personal interview, what advice she would give to young people about the future, she replied, "The only advice I will give to anyone about making tomorrow better is simply this: If you do unto others as you would have them do unto you, there will be a lot less confusion and a whole lot more understanding." Goldberg lamented the lack of caring that she saw in society. "I always thought the work of human beings was to watch out for each other," she said.

"When I started out," she recalled, "I had to live through people's ridicule of the way I looked, the way I moved, how I dressed. And I resisted other people's ideas about what I should be. People said, 'Don't do comedy, do drama.' Then they said, 'Stick to comedy.' I finally said, 'Look, I'm gonna do what I want.' It may not be materially rewarding, but heartwise it does me a lot of good. I come from an era when you were encouraged to shoot for your goals. I have a daughter and she's different because of her environment—but when you put her against the rest of the young people in this country, they

Goldberg gets a kiss from New York mayor David Dinkins after a 1989 meeting of the Creative Coalition, an organization of politically concerned entertainers. Though Goldberg's political views do not follow any party line, she has never wavered in her advocacy of humanitarian causes.

71

Goldberg rehearses with pop star Gloria Estefan for a Miami benefit concert in September 1992. The concert raised money to aid victims of Hurricane Andrew, which had devastated South Florida earlier in the month.

don't have much hope. There isn't much encouragement. People need encouragement and to feel that those points of light [a phrase used by former president George Bush] include them. Maybe we're just the backdrop against which those points of light can sparkle."

Because she sees the world as a family affair, Goldberg is active in many charities. She donates not only her money but also her time and her talent. In the autumn of 1992, for instance, a violent hurricane struck the coast of southern Florida. Thousands of people in the Miami area lost their homes and all

On Christmas Eve, 1987, Goldberg and other volunteers serve a holiday dinner to homeless people in Washington, D.C. "It's disgusting," she declared, "that we could have this beautiful country and have families living in dumpsters."

their possessions. The pop singer Gloria Estefan, a longtime Miami resident, organized a benefit concert to raise money for the victims. When Goldberg was asked to appear at the benefit, she agreed without hesitation and performed a stand-up comedy routine at the September 26 event.

A few weeks later, on October 11, she was in New York City for an AIDS benefit sponsored by the

actress Elizabeth Taylor, who has devoted much of her time and effort to fund-raising in hopes of finding a cure for the fatal disease. The $200-a-ticket event took place in Madison Square Garden; Goldberg joined such stars as Elton John and Lionel Richie in entertaining the capacity crowd.

Goldberg has received many awards for her charitable activities, which have also included campaigns

Goldberg cavorts with fellow comedians Billy Crystal and Robin Williams during a publicity session for "Comic Relief IV." Aired in 1990, the award-winning cable TV comedy special raised $6 million for the homeless.

to help young people fight drugs. In 1989, she was named Humanitarian of the Year by the Starlight Foundation, and the following year she was honored for contributions to the advancement of the status of women in the United States. In 1991, she received the Norman Zarky Humanitarian Award, sponsored by Women in Film. In 1993, Harvard University's Hasty Pudding Club gave Goldberg its Hasty Pudding Pot award for "lasting and impressive contributions to the world of entertainment." During her acceptance speech, Goldberg said, "I'd like to take us to a different place where people are known as humans, not black or white."

Jerry Zucker, who directed Goldberg's Oscar-winning performance in *Ghost*, recently reflected on the complexity of Goldberg's personality. He laughingly observed, "I can see her saying, 'Mess with me and I'll break your face.' " But behind that facade of toughness, he added, there is a tender-hearted person who really does want to change the world.

One of Goldberg's most cherished goals is to get the homeless people of America off the streets and into decent places to live. "It's disgusting," she has said, "that we could have this beautiful country and have families living in dumpsters. You can't talk about embracing a world when you don't embrace your own people."

One of the ways in which Goldberg puts her words into practice is "Comic Relief," an ongoing television benefit to aid homeless people in America that began in the 1980s. The program grew out of the vision shared by Bob Zmuda, a comedy writer, and a few of his colleagues. Along with many Americans, Zmuda could see that during the 1980s, more and more people were losing their jobs and being forced out of their homes. It might be easy to step over one homeless person on the sidewalk, but it was impossible to ignore so many people all over the country who could no longer keep a roof over their heads. Most Americans associated poverty with Third World countries. The 1980s showed that poverty was right next door.

Zmuda thought of a way to raise money and to direct attention to the plight of homeless Americans. His idea was to organize a live television show that would present the talents of America's greatest comedy stars. Comedy, reasoned Zmuda, brings millions of people some relief from their everyday cares. For this reason, "Comic Relief" was adopted as the name of the project.

Finding a name was the easy part. Actually producing the show was something else. The first problem was finding someone to put up the money.

The comedians would, of course, be expected to devote their time and talents for no pay. In return, they would be free of the censorship that a normal television broadcast imposes. Appearing on cable, without sponsors, they could be as uninhibited in their language and subject matter as they would be in a private club. Zmuda also wanted to make absolutely sure that every penny the "Comic Relief" benefit collected in donations from the public would actually get to the homeless who needed it. In other words, someone would have to foot the bill for all the costs of the production. When Zmuda convinced HBO, the largest subscription television network in America, to underwrite the venture, "Comic Relief" was under way.

The first "Comic Relief" telecast took place in 1986 and starred three equally zany personalities— Billy Crystal, Robin Williams, and Whoopi Goldberg. All three showed up looking rather natty in black tuxedos. In addition, 47 other comedians donated their time and talents to the show, which was held in the Universal Amphitheatre in Los Angeles. On that evening, "Comic Relief" raised more than $2.5 million for America's homeless. Every cent of the money went to the National Health Care for the Homeless program and was eventually distributed in 18 cities across the country.

The second benefit, in 1987, also showcased 50 comics and raised another $2.5 million. "Comic Relief III" brought in $4 million, and the 1990 benefit, held in New York's Radio City Music Hall, took in a total of $6 million. After "Comic Relief V" had been aired, the project had distributed more than $18 million in 23 cities.

On May 9, 1990, Goldberg and Williams traveled to Washington, D.C., to testify before the Senate Labor and Human Resources Committee. They urged Congress to pass the Homelessness Prevention and

Community Revitalization Act, which was designed to give long-term help to homeless families. With the help of the two celebrities, the bill became part of the Homelessness Assistance Amendments Act of 1990.

On May 11, 1991, a "Comic Relief" Night was held at Shea Stadium, home of the New York Mets baseball team. Goldberg, along with Crystal and Williams, shared the ceremonial duty of throwing out the first ball before the game. At Radio City Music Hall, the mayor of New York City, David Dinkins, presented the three comics with a proclamation in recognition of their work. When asked about her involvement in causes such as "Comic Relief," Goldberg had a quick and heartfelt response: "It's not somebody else's problem." ❧

7

GETTING INVOLVED

CONSIDERING HER DESIRE to involve herself in the lives of people less fortunate than herself, it was no surprise that Goldberg was willing to take a clear-cut political stance during the 1992 presidential campaign. Goldberg made no secret about her preferences. At the Madison Square Garden benefit for Elizabeth Taylor's AIDS Foundation, Goldberg took a few minutes before introducing Lionel Richie to urge the audience not to vote for then-president George Bush. She resented both the Reagan and Bush administrations, she said, for placing the blame for all of society's problems on everybody else. "I take great offense," she said, "when the present government tries to make us believe that our problems are all the result of old policies."

During the election campaign, she gave Bush's Democratic opponent, Bill Clinton, only a lukewarm endorsement, though she did call him on the air during her talk show to congratulate him on his overwhelming victory. After Clinton had completed his first year in office, Goldberg became an enthusiastic supporter of his social programs, especially his plan to reform the nation's health care system and provide coverage for all Americans. Though she also got to know the president personally, she was not afraid to make a few jokes at his expense during an October

In one of her most challenging film roles, Goldberg portrays a dedicated South African teacher in the 1992 film Sarafina! *Though some black radical groups criticized Goldberg for making a film in racially segregated South Africa, Goldberg believed that she was contributing to the African liberation struggle.*

81

1993 benefit performance in the president's honor at Ford's Theater in Washington.

Dropping her hard-edged persona, Goldberg admitted in a 1994 magazine interview that she was thrilled to be on such close terms with the most powerful political figure in the nation: "I mean, I'm in a great position. I get to meet amazing people. I get to hang out with the president of the United States, OK? . . . And every now and then I think back: I come from the projects, man."

Despite her wealth, Goldberg made it clear that she fully supported Clinton's determination to narrow the gap between the rich and the poor. "I could stand to give a little bit," she said. "If I say things need to change, then I have to be willing to be part of that. And if that means giving up, because I'm in that percentage that has a lot more than everybody else, I'm all for that."

Goldberg has also declared herself pro-choice on the issue of abortion rights, feeling that a woman should have the ability to choose whether or not she wishes to have a child. During a television interview, she asserted, "We're getting the names and addresses of all the anti-abortionists so when all the kids have babies we can bring the babies to them to raise." She also stated that the issue was not "whether you're for or against abortion. The issue is do you have the right to tell someone what they can or cannot do."

During the 1992 election campaign, Vice-President Dan Quayle caused a great deal of controversy with remarks that were taken as a condemnation of single mothers. Not trying to hide her anger, Goldberg spoke out. "Single parents have existed for a long time, you know," she said. "And whether a woman chooses to have a baby on her own or not, if she's a working woman, why are you concerned about it? You don't want her on welfare, and yet you don't want her to be working either."

Goldberg was able to speak with great authority on the subject of single motherhood, having been through the experience herself. She was also well qualified to speak about the welfare system, having been a recipient when she was struggling to bring up her daughter and break into show business. She is vocal in her belief that the country's "demeaning and dehumanizing" welfare system must be reformed. Another passion of Goldberg's is her campaign against drug use and her advocacy of better rehabilitation programs. She is concerned with keeping young people from suffering through the tough times she experienced.

Although Goldberg claims that she does not dwell on the subject of race or its impact on her career, she is deeply aware of her position as a well-known black woman in America. She has received a number of awards from such black organizations as the NAACP for her work on film and in television. Her awareness of how blacks are portrayed in the media led her to become involved in 1992 with the movie version of the South African musical hit, *Sarafina!* (1992). Goldberg became the first African-American actress to shoot a film in South Africa, noted for its rigid, although now officially outlawed, policy of apartheid, or strict segregation of the races. Many Africans and African Americans criticized her for agreeing to appear in the film, but for Goldberg it was a journey of self-education.

Sarafina! is the story of a young black girl in Soweto, the largest black township in South Africa. The musical, shot mainly in Soweto's Morris Isaacson School, concerns the political unrest that swept South Africa in 1976. At that time, thousands of black students rioted to protest the government's policy of apartheid. As the musical opens, Sarafina is a naive young girl who concerns herself only with her desire to be an entertainer. The story depicts

Flanked by actresses Marlo Thomas and Cybill Shepherd, Goldberg takes part in a pro-choice demonstration in Washington, D.C., in 1989. Though she did not advocate abortion, Goldberg asserted that no government or group should have the power to force a woman to bear a child.

Sarafina's life-transforming experience, during which she sees the true horrors of apartheid and joins the often violent struggle for freedom by South African blacks.

Sarafina's schoolteacher in the play is Mary, a liberal and passionate woman who tries to awaken a feeling of political consciousness in her pupils. The

film's producer, Anant Singh, wanted Goldberg for the role, but he doubted that he could persuade her to do it. However, when Goldberg read the script, she immediately said yes.

In early 1992, Goldberg found herself far from home, surrounded by 2 million black Africans as she shot scenes in the township of Soweto. For five weeks she made her own voyage of discovery through that troubled country. By day she listened as South African blacks and whites engaged in their favorite topic of conversation—politics. By night she read books in her hotel suite that recorded South Africa's tragic history. She was awed just by the contrasts in lifestyle. During the days when the film was shot, she was surrounded by the chickens, squatters' shacks, and dust of Soweto. Just 20 minutes away was the home of a white businessman who held a reception in Goldberg's honor. The $10 million house had eight bedrooms, nine baths, eight garages, two swimming pools, and a dozen rooms for the servants. It was also surrounded by a seven-foot wall.

When the film was completed and Goldberg left South Africa, she remained baffled by the continued survival of apartheid. "I just don't understand how it continues," she said. "And everybody's afraid. I can feel that. Whites are afraid because they figure if the blacks take over, they'll be hurt. But I think to myself, 'If you had treated people halfway decently, you wouldn't have to be this nervous.'"

Goldberg may have felt that she was contributing to the betterment of South African blacks by taking part in the filming of *Sarafina!* But not everyone in the country, blacks included, welcomed her. She had arrived in South Africa just after the pop singer Paul Simon completed his troubled concert tour. Even though Simon featured black African artists on his tour, some groups had threatened to disrupt his performances by violent means. They believed that no entertainers from any nation should showcase their talents in South Africa until the segregation policy was changed. These radical black organizations said that Goldberg should have stayed home, too. They denounced her in the press. Someone even stole her passport, but it turned up mysteriously just before she was to return home.

South African women demonstrate against their nation's restrictive racial laws in 1959. When Goldberg traveled to South Africa in 1992 to make Sarafina! she was struck by the contrast between the impoverished black townships and the affluent white suburbs.

Pop singer Paul Simon performs with members of the South African group Ladysmith Black Mambazo. In 1992, when the United Nations and the African National Congress ended the cultural boycott against South Africa, Simon included the troubled nation in his "Born at the Right Time" world tour.

Goldberg met privately with the black protesters. "I told them they didn't really have a problem with me. They didn't know anything about me." And she kept on working. She said later that she didn't like the radicals' tactics, but she understood their feelings. "There are four thousand small groups in South Africa. They needed some publicity so they used me."

Film critics in the United States were not particularly kind to *Sarafina!* But Goldberg was not sorry she took the role. Of the South African actors who worked on the film, she said, "These kids really want to build something here, and they all ask the same question: 'Am I as good as the guys in the States?' And they are." Of South Africa's race relations, she said cautiously, "This issue is going to be resolved some day because there's no compromise on it. But there's a lot to be worked out, and it will happen very slowly." Her words were borne out by the turmoil that developed throughout South Africa in 1993 and 1994, as the nation cautiously approached the first truly free elections in its history. The elections themselves, held at the end of April 1994, were largely peaceful and brought a massive turnout in the black townships. When the votes were tallied, Nelson Mandela, leader of the African National Congress, emerged as the first black president of South Africa, thus opening a hopeful new chapter in the nation's history.

Looking past the political aspects of her trip, Goldberg was astonished by how many South Africans had seen her movies. People would stop her on the street to comment on her performances in such films as *Ghost* or *The Long Walk Home*. But as of 1994, South Africans had still not seen Goldberg in *The Color Purple* because Alice Walker, the author of the original novel, had retained control over the film and would not allow its screening in South Africa.

Back home, Goldberg has often used her talents to improve race relations and to promote children's issues on television. Because she feels that education is the key to ending bigotry and racism and violence in this country, she has appeared on a number of children's programs, most notably "Sesame Street."

Ever since it first went on the air during the 1960s, "Sesame Street" has been both entertaining youngsters and teaching them about a variety of subjects. The program has also been dealing, in a very subtle way, with race relations. One of its messages was contained in the well-known song "It's Not Easy Being Green," sung by Kermit the Frog. Deciding to be even more direct, the producers took their cameras to the East Harlem section of New York, where they showed Hispanic-American children making masks. Other programs included a trip to the Caribbean island of Puerto Rico to see how a young boy spent his day and a feature on the life of a *charro*, a Mexican-American cowboy in Arizona. On one show, a white girl spent an overnight with her friend, a black girl living in the inner city.

Goldberg liked what "Sesame Street" was trying to do, and she made several guest appearances on the program. In one segment, Goldberg sat on a bench having a conversation with the cuddly red monster known to "Sesame Street" fans as Elmo. Goldberg and Elmo began to talk about each other's looks. "I like my red fur," Elmo declared. "I like my brown skin," Goldberg replied.

Goldberg also did the voice of Gaia, the spirit of earth, on "Captain Planet and the Planeteers," an animated environmental series that won her an Emmy nomination. She has also made recordings for children, including *Koi and the Kola Nuts*, an African folktale that she narrates. There is no question that Goldberg has been getting through to her intended audience. On four separate occasions, she has been honored with Nickelodeon's Kid's Choice Award, naming her young people's favorite movie actress.

8

"I AM WHERE I SHOULD BE"

FOLLOWING HER SUCCESSFUL debut as host of the Oscars in March 1994, Goldberg resumed her busy acting schedule. She was looking forward to the release of *Corrina, Corrina*, a family comedy set in the 1950s, in which she costarred with Ray Liotta. At the same time, she was involved in filming *Boys on the Side*, a "road" movie that also featured Mary-Louise Parker and Drew Barrymore.

Looking ahead in her career, Goldberg long ago accepted the idea that there is no particular niche for her to fill in show business. "It's kind of, like, no one's quite sure what to say about me and where to put me," she acknowledged, "so they made me a star and figured that'll cover whatever comes down." The experience of being a star is not one that she has embraced without reservation, having learned that celebrity has its downside. As she told an interviewer in 1992, "Sometimes it's fun. It's been tougher on my family than on me, because I can detach from it. I only have to be Whoopi Goldberg when I go out the door. But it's been hard on my kid. You're thirteen or fourteen and you don't know if someone likes you because you're you or they think they're going to get to your mom that way. So it's very hard on self-esteem and self-image."

At the top of her profession in the 1990s, Goldberg was eager for new challenges. "I've been the luckiest woman on the face of the earth, careerwise," she said. "If you are doing what you love, then nothing else will really matter."

Goldberg greets President Bill Clinton after a performance at Ford's Theatre in October 1993. "I get to hang out with the president of the United States," she marveled. "And every now and then I think back: I come from the projects, man."

Having gone through the experience of mother-hood, Goldberg was acutely conscious of her growth as a person. "I couldn't know how tough it was raising kids until I had mine," she said in 1987. "One day I called up my mom and said, 'I'm sorry for being such an idiot.' For my mother to have done what she did is phenomenal. We never wanted for anything. I'm realizing now that maybe what I thought was her distance was simply her taking needed space for her time and private thoughts."

Preparing to celebrate her 40th birthday in 1995, Goldberg was certainly planning to continue acting. "If there wasn't something called acting, they would probably hospitalize people like me!" she said in a 1992 magazine interview. "The giddiness and the joy of life are the moving and grooving, the exploration. That's what I've done in acting ever since I was a kid." She elaborated on this view in a private conversation in 1994: "I've been the luckiest woman on the face of the earth, careerwise. If you are doing what you love, then nothing else will really matter. If you're doing it to try to become rich and famous, you'll probably have a much harder time than if you are doing it because you have a deep desire to act or sing or dance."

Acting has provided Goldberg's greatest sense of accomplishment, but it has also been the source of her greatest frustration. Because she believes that theater and film deal with the world of make-believe, she insists that she should be offered any part she can master—Queen Elizabeth I of England, a pioneer woman in the Old West, a valley girl. But she knows that Hollywood is slow to change, and perhaps it never will. For this reason, she knows that she will have to accept scripts that are less than Oscar material. Taking a philosophical view, she realizes that stereotypes die hard and that Hollywood is only a reflection of attitudes in society: "People tend to [cast movie roles] on how they were brought up. If you weren't raised in a mixed environment, it might not occur to you that the lead character in *The Silence of the Lambs* could be black or Chinese or Hispanic. Once you understand that, it's no surprise that I'm not considered to be in a movie with Michael Douglas."

Goldberg has, however, reacted with some annoyance to those who criticize her for lending her talents to second-rate material. "I did the pictures I was offered," she once said. "Do you think I would sit around and say, 'Here's great scripts, here's lousy scripts. I'll do the lousy ones'?"

In addition to stage and screen work, Goldberg plans to continue doing books and recordings for young readers. She will also appear in many more television productions. She will certainly do additional benefits, including new editions of "Comic Relief." One of her main concerns continues to be her effect on young people. "That's the most important part of what I do," she told *Parade* magazine, "trying to preserve the self-esteem of young people. . . . They have to be reminded that the interests they have, whatever they are, or whoever they are—that they're great. That it's great to be interested in things that are quirky and different. That's mainly it. They don't need to fit in with everybody else. They don't need to be like everybody else."

In her public statements and activities, Goldberg demonstrates her conviction that it is possible to make the world a better place, if only people try hard enough. This attitude came across in a 1992 interview when Goldberg admitted that her one fear was that she might wake up one morning and find out it was all for nothing. When asked what that meant, she replied:

> I believe I'm here for a reason. And I think a little bit of the reason is to throw little torches out to the next step to lead people through the dark. When you're kind to someone in trouble, you hope they'll remember and be kind to someone else. And it'll become like a wildfire. Each person helping someone who then helps someone else, and so on. . . . And I'm afraid that I'm going to wake up one day, and the wind will be so strong that no torch can bear up to it. I think that's my biggest fear. That I won't be strong enough to keep throwing the torches. But I know I'll keep trying.

Certainly, Goldberg was not about to compromise her beliefs, her style, or her sense of humor in order to make herself popular with the show business establishment or to deflect any public resentment of her success. Speaking to *US* magazine in 1994, she summed up the unflinching attitude toward life that had shaped her remarkable career: "I believe that if you cop to your mistakes, if you say what you mean and if you mean what you say, you should be all right. And it's OK not to be necessarily well liked by people. That's all right. They'll get over it. [*Laughs*] So I just kind of feel I am where I should be."

CHRONOLOGY

———— ✿ ————

1955   Born Caryn Johnson on November 13 in New York City

1963   Begins acting with the Helena Rubinstein Performing Arts Workshops at the Hudson Guild

1969   Graduates from St. Columba School and enters Washington Irving High School

1972   Drops out of high school; checks into Horizon House for drug rehabilitation; marries her drug counselor

1973   Gives birth to daughter, Alexandrea

1974   Divorces husband; moves to San Diego, California, with her daughter

1976   Joins San Diego Repertory Theater

1979   Moves to Berkeley and joins Blake Street Hawkeyes

1983   Gains recognition in New York City with *The Spook Show*

1984   *Whoopi Goldberg* opens on Broadway

1985   Goldberg receives Academy Award nomination for Best Actress for Steven Spielberg's *The Color Purple*; wins Grammy Award for best comedy recording, *Whoopi Goldberg: Direct from Broadway*

1986   Stars in *Jumpin' Jack Flash*; cohosts the first "Comic Relief" benefit for the homeless with Robin Williams and Billy Crystal; receives Emmy Award nomination for Best Guest Performer in a Dramatic Series for "Moonlighting"

1987   Featured in *Burglar* and *Fatal Beauty*

1988   Nominated for an American Comedy Award as Funniest Female Performer in a TV Special for "Carol, Carl, Whoopi, and Robin"; performs leading role in *Clara's Heart*; receives Ace Award nomination for HBO's "Whoopi Goldberg's Fontaine"

1990   Costars with Sissy Spacek in *The Long Walk Home*; plays crucial supporting role in *Ghost*; testifies before a Senate committee on behalf of the homeless

1991   Wins Academy Award as Best Supporting Actress for *Ghost*; writes children's book, *Alice*; gives another comedic turn in *Soapdish*

1992   Stars in the highly successful comedy *Sister Act* and the South African musical drama *Sarafina!*; appears in Robert Altman's *The Player*; hosts a late-night TV talk show; receives Emmy Award as Outstanding Actress in a Drama Series, Television Movie or Mini-Series for "Star Trek: The Next Generation"; wins an Ace Award for "Comic Relief V"; becomes first female host of the Grammy Awards

1993   Costars with Ted Danson in *Made in America*; becomes one of Hollywood's highest-paid performers with the release of *Sister Act 2: Back in the Habit*

1994   Hosts the 66th Annual Academy Awards

FURTHER READING

Blum, David. "Whoa." *Esquire*, February 1985.

Contreras, Joseph. "Caught in the Cross-fire." *Newsweek*, January 20, 1992.

Erickson, Steve. "Whoopi Goldberg." *Rolling Stone*, May 8, 1986.

Hine, Darlene Clark, ed. *Black Women in America: An Historical Encyclopedia*. Vol. 1. Brooklyn, NY: Carlson Publishing, 1993.

Martin, Linda, and Kerry Seagrave. *Women in Comedy*. New York: Citadel, 1986.

Randolph, Laura B. "The Whoopi Goldberg Nobody Knows." *Ebony*, March 1991.

Skow, John. "The Joy of Being Whoopi." *Time*, September 21, 1992.

Wenner, Jan S. "This Sister's Act." *US*, April 1994.

"Whoopi Goldberg." *People Weekly*, December 28, 1992.